SECRET PLACE
of the
MOST HIGH

Tony M. Carpenter

The Secret Place of The Most High

Copyright @2023 Tony M. Carpenter

ISBN 979-8-8520-3877-7

For more information about the author or to contact him please visit: Riverchurchbaltimore@gmail.com

Contents

Psalm 91 (AMPC)

1   He who dwells in the secret place of the Most High
    shall remain stable and fixed under the shadow of
    the Almighty [Whose power no foe can withstand].

2   I will say of the Lord, He is my Refuge and my
    Fortress, my God; on Him I lean and rely, and in
    Him I [confidently] trust!

3   For [then] He will deliver you from the snare of the
    fowler and from the deadly pestilence.

4   [Then] He will cover you with His pinions, and
    under His wings shall you trust and find refuge;
    His truth and His faithfulness are a shield and a
    buckler.

5   You shall not be afraid of the terror of the night,
    nor of the arrow (the evil plots and slanders of the
    wicked) that flies by day,

6   Nor of the pestilence that stalks in darkness, nor
    of the destruction and sudden death that surprise
    and lay waste at noonday.

7   A thousand may fall at your side, and ten thou-
    sand at your right hand, but it shall not come near
    you.

8   Only a spectator shall you be [yourself inaccessible in the secret place of the Most High] as you witness the reward of the wicked.

9   Because you have made the Lord your refuge, and the Most High your dwelling place,

10   There shall no evil befall you, nor any plague or calamity come near your tent.

11   For He will give His angels [especial] charge over you to accompany and defend and preserve you in all your ways [of obedience and service].

12   They shall bear you up on their hands, lest you dash your foot against a stone.

13   You shall tread upon the lion and adder; the young lion and the serpent shall you trample underfoot.

14   Because He has set his love upon Me, therefore will I deliver Him; I will set Him on high, because He knows and understands My name [has a personal knowledge of My mercy, love, and kindness—trusts and relies on Me, knowing I will never forsake Him, no, never].

15   He shall call upon Me, and I will answer him; I will be with him in trouble, I will deliver him and honor him.

16   With long life will I satisfy him and show him My salvation.

CHAPTER 1

In the Secret Place, You Don't Have to Be Afraid of Anything

*P*salm 91 gives us the keys to walking in God's protection, provision, victory and more. We are called to walk in the supernatural. This means we are not meant to be confined to the limitations of this fallen world.

However, there is something we must do in order to see His power and promises in our lives.

A lot of preaching and theology has been done to try to make sense of why so many often see the opposite of what the Bible states they can have. People are often taught to passively accept it when they don't see what the Bible says. However, if we are going to have God's best for our lives, we will have to contend for it. The promises of God are not automatic. If we don't grasp this, we can find ourselves defeated in life and actually think this is normal. For example, some people say, "I'm just passing through life. Sometimes you get curveballs. Sometimes you win; sometimes you lose." I don't accept that. I am going to believe the Bible. If the Bible says it, I am going to believe it. Some people also say, "You've got to go through the valley before you get to the mountain, and then you have got to go back to the valley." The issue with that is we are not talking about geography; this is the Bible. The Bible says" ... the path of the just is like the shining sun, That shines ever brighter unto the perfect day." *Proverbs 4:18 (NKJV)* Will things try to shake you? Yes. But as you learn to dwell in God's presence, you will overcome every obstacle and become unshakable. In the secret place everything that opposes you must bow. For example, I once watched a video in which some thieves were coming to rob two women. However, these were two Holy Ghost women, and they took their Bibles out. Although I could not see everything in the video, I could read their lips. As one guy tried to grab one of the lady's purses, she said, "In the name of Jesus." The guy who grabbed the purse began to rock back and forth and then fell to his knees. You do not mess with somebody in the secret place. That is a warning to your enemies, and they have to back up. You have authority, God's presence, and angels when you walk in that place.

Angels to protect you

In the Bible, just one angel destroyed 185,000 people (See *2 Kings 19:35*), and the Bible says He will give His angels company over you. You may have one or two angels, or you may live in a certain area and have four or five. Think about that. Imagine driving down the highway and a car tries to get in the way, but the angels come and intervene. Even if you can't see it, the angels are there. You can be confident in Christ when you are in the secret place. You can go wherever God tells you to go with angels to guard you.

You are unstoppable when you live sold out for Jesus and walk in His presence. You can go to places normal people should not go, take ground for the kingdom, and walk away unscathed. There have been many times where I could have died, but I was protected. In the office of an evangelist, you go to places you should not go. You say things you probably should not say, and then you encounter certain people who you normally would not encounter.

One day I was out putting out flyers for an event, and I was in a very rough area. I went to place a flyer on a door and as soon as I did, I heard loud music, so I was about to walk away. As I was walking, suddenly the Lord said, "Turn around and go knock on the door."

I turned around and went to do as the Lord told me. The moment I knocked, a very intimidating man answered, and just as he opened the door, a puff of smoke came out. One look inside and I knew it was a place where they were dealing drugs.

As I walked in, there was a TV, a radio, a plastic table, and about four or five big football- player-type, mean-looking men. I was definitely the smallest guy there. I looked like I was in elementary school going to a high school football game. It felt like Goliath versus David. Suddenly, the guy who answered shut the door with me inside.

Now I am there with these guys looking at me, and I decide that it is time to pray in emergency tongues. They asked, "What do you want?" I said that I didn't know.

However, what I did know is that if you are not sure what to do, then start preaching. So, suddenly, I just started to preach like I was at a crusade with 10,000 people.

If it wasn't for the Lord, these guys would have eaten me for breakfast. They would have rolled me up in a taco and devoured me. It would have been deep-fried Pastor Tony, but God was with me. As I was preaching, one of the guys turned the music down and suddenly, the glory of God started filling the room, and a boldness came over me. I quickly had a new confidence that was not there before. Now you could tell these guys were in a gang, but after I got done, they said, "Man, thank you so much."

One of them wanted to slide a bunch of money to me and said it was for the church. I said, "No, I'm good; everything is great." He insisted, but I told him I was good and asked if he could open the door so I could leave. He let me out, and I safely walked away.

That is a true story. As I walked out, suddenly this thought came to mind, "Oh, my God, I could have died back there." The Lord then gave me the promise: "…I'll give my angels charge over you wherever you go." (See *Psalm 91:11*). As you abide in the secret place, these angels supernaturally protect you wherever you go.

That is why you do not have to be afraid of anything. I am telling you that you can be fearless. Not stupid, but fearless. If you say, "Pastor, let's go jump out of planes." Well, that is stupid. You do not want to go home early for being stupid. What we are talking about is walking in the secret place of the Most High.

CHAPTER 2

What is the Secret Place?

I want you to get this in your spirit. Just because you are in church, does not mean you are in the secret place. Just because you are serving in church, and you have a title does not mean you are in the secret place. Just because you are called Pastor or Bishop or Elder or Deacon or Prophetess does not mean that you are in the secret place. There is a place to get into with God, where life literally becomes like heaven on earth.

It is not complicated

Contrary to what most people think, the Bible is not confusing. It is very simple. Jesus said: "And you shall love the Lord your God with all your heart, with all your soul, with all your mind, and with all your strength. This is the first commandment. And the second, like it, is this: 'You shall love your neighbor as yourself.' There is no other commandment greater than these." *Mark 12:30-31 (NKJV)*. Do you know what the secret place is? It is being fully intoxicated in love with God and making Him number one in your life. That is how to live, abide, and remain in the secret place. This is where the angels come in. That is where no evil will befall you. That is where no plague will ever come nigh your dwelling. That is where you will tread upon the lion and the adder. The young dragon you will trample under your foot when you walk in this place.

I watched a movie once called Bubble Boy. It was about a boy who due to a lack of an immune system had to stay within this bubble suit that was specially designed for him. What was so amazing to me is that the outside could not affect him as long as he stayed within the bubble suit. That is exactly how the secret place works, and there God literally becomes a shield around you. You can get under the covering of God where the heat does not affect you anymore. Have you ever been on the beach and forgot to put on sunscreen, and you turned into a tomato? You are in the sun, and you do not even realize it until you get home. You start feeling your skin all burnt up because you were not under a covering. Similarly, when it rains, everybody always goes for an umbrella, particularly women. If it starts raining, my wife will not get out of the car without an umbrella. I want to just go, but my wife wants a covering.

Psalm 91 tells us the place where you can be under God's covering. There is a place where you can be under the pavilion of God. Scripture states: "The name of the Lord *is* a strong tower; The righteous run to it and are safe." *Proverbs 18:10 (NKJV)*

All things working for your good

I am talking about being in Christ, and God being your everything. When you are in that pavilion, everything seems to work out and click like dominoes. When you are under the shadow, you are always in the right place at the right time. The Bible says all things work together for good, and people just stop reading there. It actually says, "And we know that all things work together for good to those who love God, to those who are the called according to His purpose." *Romans 8:28 (NKJV).* If I am in God's purpose and I love God, I can make a statement that says all things are working together for my good because I meet the conditions. There is a covering that is heaven on earth if you can stay in it. Every day you wake up, and God works your situations out. Jesus said: "The thief cometh not, but for to steal, and to kill, and to destroy: I am come that they might have life, and that they might have it more abundantly." *John 10:10 (KJV).* You do not need alcohol. You do not need fornication. You do not need those things to get through life. You can just get under the covering of God.

Stay in His hiding place

My oldest daughter, Zoe, loves to play hide-and-go seek. One day my family and I are walking around shopping and Zoe decides to hide. Suddenly, I don't see her with us, and I ask my wife, "Is Zoe with you?" She said that she wasn't. All of us, including my other girls, started calling for her. I am going down one aisle after another. Then I felt the

Holy Spirit say, "Go back to where you first started." So, I go back there and everything bad that could happen is going through my head. Then a couple tells us she is in the coat rack, and I open it up and there is Zoe. We were freaking out, and Zoe is sitting back there laughing her head off. She was hidden and inaccessible to us.

See, that is what happens. Demons try to harm you, but they can't find you. Devils are looking and wanting to devour you, but they can't because you are in the secret place. You are hidden, so they can't touch you. The devil cannot override where God is. That is why he is away from God. In Genesis when God came and kicked Adam and Eve out of the garden, an angel with a flaming sword stood in front of the entrance, and they could not get in. They had no access. But guess what? Jesus came down on the earth and tore the veil to the Holy of Holies apart and left. Now by His Spirit, He wants to live on the inside of people. That's why it says, "Behold I stand at the door and knock..." *Revelation 3:20* (NKJV). People say they are looking for God, and they ask where He is. He is standing at the door of your heart, and He is knocking. He says," I want to come in. I want to have a relationship with you."

Who do you want to meet with?

There are so many people who always want to meet the big shot. We all want to meet certain people. There are certain pastors and ministers I would love to meet or have lunch with, but how much more the Lord? Some wait in line for hours to meet famous people. Back in the day, people would go crazy to meet Michael Jackson. Maybe today it is Justin Bieber, but there is a God who actually wants to meet with you. The Bible says, "What is man, that thou art mindful of him?" *Psalm 8:4 (KJV)*. The angels are in awe and wonder as to why we are the apple of His eye. Why would He come into a human body and die for us? They wonder at how God wants a relationship with us, and how He wants us more than we wanted Him. They watch as people open up and fully put their everything in God. They are astounded at how people's lives change completely, and the windows of heaven open over them.

There is no one greater to know than God, and He wants to dine with you. Do not keep Him waiting.

CHAPTER 3

The Secret to Success in the Kingdom of God

Do you realize there is a benefit to being sold out to God?

W hen you are sold out to God, you will see things happen in your life that you never dreamed possible. God wants all of us, but in return He gives us all of Himself and that includes His favor, protection, and blessings. Here are some examples of men in the Bible who sold out and what God did with them.

DAVID

> *1 Samuel 2:8 (NKJV)* states God took David out of the ash heap and made him a king. The Bible in one translation says the dunghill (see *1 Samuel 2:8 KJV*). He was literally sitting in dung. Then God, because of his relationship in the secret place set David up, and he became

the greatest king in Israel's history and part of Jesus' earthly lineage.

DANIEL

Daniel was a slave and became a great prophet who even foretold the events of the end of time, the great tribulation, the antichrist, and more.

PAUL

Paul was a persecutor of the church and a pharisee who became the greatest of the apostles and writer of two-thirds of the New Testament.

MOSES

Moses, raised by Pharaoh, was a man who had a heart toward God and His people. He was used to deliver Israel from slavery, part the Red Sea, write the first five books of the Bible and more. The scripture says he was the most humble man in all the earth. (See *Numbers 12:3 NKJV*)

ABRAHAM

He was a man with no children who became a father when he was one-hundred-years old. He had countless descendants as God promised. He, through his obedience, was called a friend of God and is called the Father of Faith.

I can go down the list of people who seemed like the least likely candidates, but had a heart toward God, and as a result, God used them.

See, that is what God is looking for.

Remember, God is looking for a man after His own heart (see *1 Sam 13:14 KJV*). That is why religious people cannot flow with me because religion focuses purely on the outward. They say, "Oh, that guy has tattoos," but they do not know I got them before I got saved. Others may say, "Well, God can't use you; you did drugs." God can use anybody. He is actually after the heart. Many people can look at you from the outside. They can look at the divorce. They can look at what happened to you. You went to jail, but they do not know your heart. That is why God picked you. God picks the heart, not the outside. You might say, "Well, Pastor, I failed miserably."

Ok, but guess what? So did other people. But when you get your heart right with God and you sell out to the King, He can do things for you that will astound those around you. People will ask, "Why is he getting to do that?" Well, because sometimes favor is not fair. We see what is happening outside, but we do not know what a person is doing in private.

What did Jesus constantly call the Pharisees? He called them hypocrites because they dressed nicely; they knew how to say good prayers on the street corner, but inwardly they were devils. What did Jesus tell us? He said, "And when you pray, you shall not be like the hypocrites. For they love to pray standing in the synagogues and on the corners of the streets, that they may be seen by men. Assuredly, I say to you, they have their reward. But you, when you pray, go into your room, and when you have shut your door, pray to your Father who *is* in the secret *place;* and your Father who sees in secret will reward you openly. *Matthew 6:5-6 (NKJV).*

Religion is acting like you love God, but really loving other things. It is so easy to put on appearances in church. I am not trying to be negative; I am just being honest. But God says if you will be with Him in secret and look for His approval, not man's, He will reward you and do so publicly.

Who killed Jesus? It was religious folks. It was people who say they love the God of Abraham, Isaac, and Jacob, but they did not even realize that God himself was in their midst. Jesus had to go outside the church to find people. His ministry was more outside than inside. *John 1:11-12 (NKJV)* says: "He came to His own, and His own did not receive Him. But as many as received Him, to them He gave the right to become children of God, to those who believe in His name."

Matthew 23:37 (NKJV) says, "O Jerusalem, Jerusalem, the one who kills the prophets and stones those who are sent to her! How often I wanted to gather your children together, as a hen gathers her chicks under her wings, but you were not willing!"

What is He saying about Jerusalem? He is stating He wants to cover them. He wants to bring them under His shadow, but they won't come. See, you can know the Bible, but you need to know the author of the Bible. People can quote the Greek words and the Hebrew words and that is great, but do people actually know the author of the Bible?

Have they learned scripture but never come under the covering?

Religion can quote scripture, but there is not one ounce of relationship. See, relationship is everything. You are either in religion or you are in relationship. I will say it again. You are either in religion or you are in relationship. You can be married but not have a marriage. It is a fact. I know a couple (this was years ago) where the husband would sleep upstairs, and the wife would live in the basement, yet they have the title of marriage. However, there is no relationship. The husband does not respond. He does not open the door or buy flowers for her like he used to. The excitement and passion are gone.

Revelation Chapter 2 talks about returning to your first love. Then to the Laodicean church in Chapter 3, He said you are not hot, and you are not cold, but you are lukewarm. Lukewarm is being religious, carrying a Bible big enough to choke a moose, saying all the right religious words, "Amen, Brother. Praise the Lord." But it can become repetitive. With religion we have our set service, we sing, we preach, then maybe run around, and do an altar call. Then after that is over, we go out to eat and then do nothing all day. You look passionate for God in church, but it leaves once you are outside.

Do not lose your fire

You must be very careful that you do not fall into ritual and religion. You must stay intimate with God. You have got to keep the fire burning. The prophet Moses told the Levites: "Remember, the fire must be kept burning on the altar at all times. It must never go out." *Leviticus 6:13 (NLT)*. He said to keep the altar burning like the Olympics keeps the torch burning. If your fire ever goes out, it is because you were not in the secret place. You need to be aware that the devil is after your fire. The Bible says you are "the salt of the earth" *(Matthew 5:13)* and "the light of the world" *(5:14 both NKJV)*. If the devil can take your light out, then there is just darkness.

Salt is useless if it loses its saltiness. You put salt in the water, and it is gone. So, the devil is after taking the light and the salt out. The devil does not want people to be intimate with God. He does not mind if you go to church, but he does mind if you are on fire. He does not want you going home to read your Bible and lying on the carpet, crying out to the Lord. He wants you on Facebook. He does not mind if you do a little, tiny prayer in the church. The moment you start really getting into praying in the Spirit, though, he gets scared. He knows at that point you are entering into another realm of being a threat to him. I pray this message will stir you up to go turn on some worship music and seek Him. I believe many will read this and put the distractions down to spend more time with Him. It is time to get back to how we sought God before we had so many cares of life to take away our focus.

Staying in your first love

When I first got saved, I wanted the church to be open every night. I wanted to be there all the time and believed God for everything. When you first get saved, you believe anything. If the Bible said Jonah swallowed the whale, you would believe it. You would be willing to go to a graveyard to raise the dead. You have such a fire. It is like when you first met your spouse. You were never saying, "Well, it's eight o'clock and, you know, we've got to get home."

No, I fell asleep one time while talking to my wife on the phone, and my ear was sweating. I was in Florida; it is humid, and my phone got stuck to my ear. That is how long I talked to her. I had fallen asleep, and she said, "Tony, are you sleeping?" I woke up and even though I was tired, instead of going to bed, I just stayed on the phone. All I wanted was more time with her.

There is an intimacy that happens when you first abide. My challenge to you is to turn it up. Do not ignore God's call to draw near. This is where the secret of your success lies. Your marriage and finances are going to succeed because of the secret place. Even your health and your body will succeed. The root of success is the secret place. Your children will be serving God because of your intimacy with Him. If I decide to get out of the secret place and go into the world, do you realize the destruction that would happen to me and my family's life?

That is why I must run to that place where every day it is about the Lord. It is not about me. God is not on my "when I get to it list." The only time some people call on God is when they don't have money for their bills, or they got sick, or they are in court. For some people, it is the jail cell or even death row. Or they call on Jesus because it is the end of the month. It's "Lord Jesus, help!!!" But on the first of the month that changes. Then they get a check, and they forget about God again. That was a lot of us back in the day, but we have been redeemed. Amen.

Do not be a gold digger

If we look at the children of Israel, God brought them out of Egypt to the wilderness to meet with them. However, they just wanted His blessings and promises and did not see it as a place of intimacy. They wanted God only if He was doing what they wanted. They didn't understand that the wilderness was not a place of destruction, it was a place to get them outside of the world and get them into the presence of God. The place of the wilderness was getting them away from city life. It was getting them away from idols, stripping things away. That's why He said: "Let my people go, so they can worship me in the wilderness..." *Exodus 7:16 (NLT)* God was saying that He wanted to send them to a land of milk and honey, a land where they dig copper and gold. But before they got to that land, He wanted them to get His heart. Do you know why the first generation wandered for forty years and most never saw the promised land? Because they could not figure out how to get into the secret place. When Moses was in the secret place, they were in the flesh. That is why Moses came down and broke the Ten Commandments. He got angry when he saw these people making gods. They were worshiping false gods. They were in the flesh. God took them out of Egypt, but Egypt was still in them.

Ask yourself this question: What if the children of Israel would have just humbled themselves and worshiped God? Perhaps they could have said, "God, we worship you. We don't know what you are doing, but we know that you are a good God. We know that you want to take us to a place, but we really want you and the rest is a reward." If they would have had that attitude, things would have been much different for them.

Sadly, Israel had become gold diggers, not God seekers. In case you do not know what that means, a gold digger is somebody who only pretends to love someone because they have the gold. Some people get around others, not because they want a relationship with them, but because they want what they have. That is basically what Israel was doing.

I am not after blessings; blessings are after me. I am after God's heart. I do not mind God's hand in my life, but I am after His heart. I want His heart because He was there when no one was there. When everybody gave up on me and I didn't know what to do, Jesus came in and set me free. He changed my life. He gave me the peace that passes all understanding. He picked me up out of jail, out of drugs. I owe Him my life. I know He will bless me but I'm not like, "Well, God, if I do that, how much are you going to bless me?" No, I do not think like that. Do you know that the secret of success in the kingdom is having a heart-driven after God? It is loving God more than you love everything else. For the women, loving God like you loved Barbie dolls back when you were little. For the men, loving God like you loved dirt bikes or sports. Many people have an object that they love or want more than anything. Rather than wanting to touch the hem of His garment, they want to touch the hem of some material possession. God is looking for people who want to touch Him. And that is why some people get accelerated. They get advanced because their heart is after Him and not just things. As you seek God for who He is and delight yourself in Him, He will give you the desires of your heart.

CHAPTER 4

The Presence of God is Greater Than Gold and Silver

The Bible talks about the deceitfulness of riches. It says: "Now he who received seed among the thorns is he who hears the word, and the cares of this world and the deceitfulness of riches choke the word, and he becomes unfruitful." *Matthew 13:22 (NKJV).*

It is not wrong to have money. God wants us to prosper. We, however, can't allow money to control us. Our first love must stay with Jesus.

We must remember if it wasn't for Jesus, we would not have anything. As nice as it is to have money, nothing can satisfy like the presence of God. After all, what makes heaven heavenly? It is His presence. The presence of God is greater than anything. Look at all the celebrities. They have everything that we think we want. They have houses; they have planes. They have chains; they have purses; they have shoes. They can eat at any top restaurant, and they are still miserable because they do not have what really matters. If you do not have God's presence, you are bankrupt.

The presence of God is greater than gold, greater than any relationship you could have. Greater than any house you could have. A great man of God who I know once said that he would rather have the presence of God for a short period than a wall of gold wrapped around the world with his name on every brick. Just a little of His presence is better than gold. That is why the Bible says, "Oh, taste and see that the LORD is good; ..." *Psalm 34:8 (NKJV).* I am here to provoke you to get back to that secret place. Get in the place where the angels are covering you, where no evil comes to you, and you trample on the enemy. Get to that place where you dominate with perpetual victory. You can be in what we call "the holy elevator." God elevates you so high that you look down on battles, and you just laugh about it. You laugh at the storms of life. They do not affect you anymore because you are covered in the secret place. You are with your Father. You are in the position of a king, and you are ruling and reigning in Christ. You might be in this world, but you are not of this world. And you are going higher and higher to a place where God wants to bring you. It is called "the sweet spot." Have you ever played in the batting cage or the driving range? Do you know when you hit the sweet spot? It is when the bat hits the ball at the perfect angle, and you can feel the power behind your swing. That is what it is like being in the secret place. Everything you touch just works. God is working miraculously in your life, and you go home and talk about all that God did. You have a whole adventure. You tell your spouse at night how God gave you favor, blessed you, and opened a door no man could have opened. Then when someone asks, "What is your secret?" You just tell them about how you are spending more time with the Lord, seeking His face, and surrendering to His will.

Safety in perilous times

I pray that this will cause a stirring in your heart because Matthew 24 talks about the last days. There will be pestilence. There will be famines. There will be earthquakes. There will be wars and rumors of wars. If you think there will not be some wars, well, they are going to happen. If you think there is not going to be more pestilence, get ready. There will be more pestilence, and there will be famines. I know people do not want to hear this, but it is what Jesus said. It is right in the Word. Some say, "Everything is going to be great; there is nothing to worry about." Yes, in the secret place. That is the great thing. As long as I am abiding in Christ, God will make a way where there seems to be no way. If food runs out in the secret place, we will call it down from heaven. We will be eating manna in the church. I am asking the Lord if He can rain down some chicken wings with some blue cheese or ranch. After all, anything is possible.

Famines, pestilences, turmoil, wars, rumors of wars. This is what is going to happen, and the Bible says men's hearts are going to fail. That's why He said in *Luke 18:1 (NLT)* "...that they should always pray and never give up." Then later He says, "...But when the Son of Man returns, how many will he find on the earth who have faith?" *Luke 18:8 (NLT)*. Will

He find people still in the secret place even though all hell is breaking loose? The governments are being shaken right now. One world religion. One world military. That is why you have seen the whole agenda with the vaccine. This was a precursor to the mark. They are getting ready for the time when you cannot buy or sell without a mark. Read the book of Revelation. That is the time that we are approaching right now, that if you do not take the mark, you cannot buy or sell.

Look at the Prophet Elijah. Ravens came and brought food to him day and night. He was in the secret place, so he knew where to go and how to access it. See, when you are in that place, you have provision that people outside cannot access.

Too busy for the wedding

Matthew 22:1-5 (NKJV) talks of three disobedient servants, and it says: "The kingdom of heaven is like a certain king who arranged a marriage for his son, and sent out his servants to call those who were invited to the wedding; and they were not willing to come. Again, he sent out other servants, saying, 'Tell those who are invited "See, I have prepared my dinner; my oxen and my fatted cattle *are* killed, and all things are ready. Come to the wedding. But they made light of it and went their ways, one to his own farm, another to his business."

One decided not to heed the king's voice and decided his farm was more important. Another went to his business and decided that making money was his priority. Then in verses 6-8, it says: " And the rest seized his servants, treated them spitefully, and killed them. But when the king heard about it, he was furious. And he sent out his armies and destroyed those murderers and burned up their city." Then he said to his servants: "The wedding is ready, but those who were invited were not worthy." *Matthew 22:6-8 (NKJV)*. They did not want to come under the cover. He is talking here about the Jewish people. Now we love Jewish people, but they are not under the covering. You say, "Well, I'm not a Jew." You are now if you have been adopted. The lesson we must take from this parable is that we can never see anything in life above heeding God's call to draw near to Him. He is extending the call to come under his protec-tion, but we must choose to heed that call. This invitation extends whether you are black, white, brown or anything else. People get stuck on skin color. They say, "Well, I'm black and I'm the royal race." or "I'm white and we are superior." No. There is no color in the kingdom. Or they say I am from this or that tribe. You do not know what tribe you are from. Have you been born again? Then you have been blood-washed. We are all the same on the inside. We all bleed red on the inside. If you are in the Kingdom, you have Kingdom privilege. You have a Kingdom card now. Favor is on your life. Blessings and prosperity are yours. Healing and deliverance are yours. Angels encamp around you. You are in the Kingdom now.

In the last part of the parable, we see a man who tries to enter into the wedding feast, but what he hears from the king shocks him. It says: "But when the king came in to see the guests, he saw a man there who did not have on a wedding garment. So, he said to him, 'Friend, how did you come in here without a wedding garment?' And he was speechless. Then the king said to the servants, 'Bind him hand and foot, take him away, and cast *him* into outer darkness; there will be weeping and gnashing of teeth.' "For many are called, but few *are* chosen." *Matthew 22:11-14 (NKJV)*. He would represent someone who professed Jesus, even went to church, but still was not covered.

True and false believers

There are people in the church who are like the man in the parable. They do not have a wedding garment. They are in church, but they are not in Christ. You know Jesus is going to blow the trumpet, and there are going to be people who are so-called Christians that are not going to make it. It is true. Matthew 25 explains all of that: the sheep and the goats, the wise and the foolish, the talents, the servants. All of these things are in the parables. Matthew 25 tells you a depiction of the church-that some people will be ready and other people won't. You need to be in the secret place. Your relationship does not need to be built off religion or me. It needs to be built off Jesus.

As a true shepherd, my goal is not for you to come and kiss my ring or bow down and kiss my shoe. No, I'm telling you to bow before Jesus. There was a prophet who I saw, and people were giving him an offering. A man came and gave an offering, got on his knees, and kissed him on the foot. I watched it and the prophet did not say anything about it. I would have kicked that guy right in the face. I would have said, "Get off me; don't you bow before me." Some say it is culture. No, it might be their culture, but it is not kingdom culture. There is a good example with John and the angel on the Island of Patmos. When John went up to heaven, he got on his knees and the angel of the Lord picked him up. He said: "...No, don't worship me. I am a servant of God, just like you and your brothers the prophets, as well as all who obey what is written in this book. Worship only God!" *Revelation 22:9 (NLT)*.

I am not trying to build a relationship based on me. I am trying to get you closer to Jesus. I am telling you there is someone who you really want to meet, and He wants to meet more with you than you want to meet with Him. There are people who think that if only they can make a business connection with Bill Gates or Donald Trump, then they would be a high roller. But someone far greater than that wants to meet with us. The creator of heaven and earth wants you to connect with Him. You can come to meet with Him, and He actually will come and meet with you! He will show up. He will come to your house. He will show up in your dreams. He will tell you what to do, where to go, who to marry, what job to get. He will give you direction. You will get a true prophetic word that no man can take from you.

CHAPTER 5

Promises in Psalm 91

*P*salm 91 has an amazing list of promises for any believer who comes to live in His presence. In this chapter, I will proceed to show all the promises and privileges available to us as children of the King.

#1: God will rescue you and deliver you from every disease.

"For [then] He will deliver you from the snare of the fowler and from the deadly pestilence." *Psalm 91:3 (AMPC)*

The first promise in Psalm 91 is really two in one. First, it says God will rescue you. Then it says God will deliver you from every disease. You may be in a bind right now. Well, guess what? He will rescue you. The scripture states: "Surely He shall deliver you from the snare of the fowler and the perilous pestilence." *Psalm 91:3 (NKJV)*

If you have a broken marriage, God can rescue that marriage. If you have a kid that is wayward, in the secret place you can pray, and God will rescue that person.

Oh, Hallelujah! To rescue means to deliver or cause to escape. God can rescue you. When I am in that place, if there are any problems, God always rescues me.

Also, if you are sick in your body, and the doctors give you no hope, God can deliver you from any disease. There are countless true stories of God delivering people from diseases no pill or procedure can cure. God can heal you under the shadow of His wing. No disease is too big. If it is Aids, Cancer, or Crohn's disease, it does not matter. There is divine health for you.

#2: God will cover you.

"[Then]He will cover you with His pinions, and under His wings shall you trust and find refuge; His truth and His faithfulness are a shield and a buckler." *Psalm 91:4 (AMPC)*

The second promise is that God will cover you. To cover something is to protect it. Protection comes by dwelling in the secret place. You do not mess with the child of God inside the secret place. If anyone messes with you, they mess with God.

Some people messed with me when I was a kid, and my dad found out. It did not end well for them. In one situation, there was a guy putting signs out in our driveway. My friends and I decided to ride our Mongoose Mountain bikes right over the sign, and that guy slammed his brakes. It was in our front yard anyway, so it was our property, but whatever. The guy hits the reverse, comes back, and it is me and about six kids. We all ran into the backyard. Do you know where I ran to? I ran to Papa.

My dad was knocked out, watching the news in his chair with a plate of food on his lap, and I ran into the house and yelled, "Dad!"

He answered, "What?"

I screamed, "Dad, there's a crazy guy in the backyard trying to kill us."

Now at this time, he was not saved. My Dad went nuts. He got up and said, "WHAT?!"

It was like I woke up a giant Alaskan bear. Through the window he saw the guy chasing the kids in the backyard. You do not go into the backyard of another man's house. You don't do it, especially in some places. My dad saw him and yelled, "Hey, what are you doing?" Suddenly, my dad doesn't talk; he just started beating him, hitting him on the back of the head. The guy started running. First, he was running this way, and then I saw him running that way. I'm like, "Go, Dad, don't mess with me!" and this guy is running and just trying to get away. My dad is clotheslining him, elbow jabbing him - you name it. I mean he was using full force, doing everything he could to attack this guy. The guy who was chasing us jumped, literally, inside the car window with his feet sticking out, and my dad was beating his feet as they took off. I am standing there with my dad, who is huffing and puffing. Then suddenly, the kids in the neighborhood start popping out saying, "Yo, your dad's nuts." I said, "That's my dad. Don't mess with me. I'll call my dad on you."

To be clear, I am not advocating for anyone to get involved with violence. I am just giving an example to illustrate that if my earthly dad protects me like that, how much more will your heavenly Father protect you. God will beat down your enemies before your face.

When you are in the secret place, people start slandering your name, but they don't realize they are only destroying themselves. That is why you must pray for your enemies. They tried to throw Shadrach, Meshach, and Abednego into the fire. Others threw Daniel in the lion's den. What happened? Daniel got out of the lion's den, and the people who threw him in got thrown in themselves, and the lions destroyed them. The three Hebrew boys got thrown into the fire but came out without even the smell of smoke. The people who picked them up to throw them in got incinerated instead. Now I know that this is not in some kids' books or even church books. They take that out, but it is in the Bible. The people who threw Daniel in the lion's den became the lion's meat. The people who tried to burn Shadrach, Meshach, and Abednego got burned up themselves.

Protection comes when you're in the secret place. As long as I remain there, I don't have to worry about demons, demons have to worry about me. Some churches are so focused on demons and principalities. You do not have to be focused on that. You did not see Peter and Paul talking about demons the whole time. They did not. They just kept going where God told them to go, and in that there is victory. Just keep moving. Do not worry about your opponent. You worry about staying fit to beat your opponent.

In sports, a team could look at their opponents and say, "Oh, man, they're practicing right now, man. They're training more than normal." But a good coach would tell them not to worry and just stay on their game. You can be so worried about what the enemy is doing that you almost get to a place of defeat.

There are certain people that I talk to, and they talk about all the evil things evil men in high places are plotting. They send me videos about some catastrophic event. Then later they talk about another one. You can hear the fear in their voice. It isn't wrong to know what is going on, but some people get so deep in conspiracy theories that they just lose their mind. People have literally gone crazy because they kept watching conspiracy theorists on the internet.

The right focus

They say "The government is contaminating the water, the land, and the air. Killer ants are coming. It will mess your head up listening to all these conspiracy people. Later in this book, I will talk about some of the things that really are happening and what our response should be, but the wicked deeds of men cannot be our main focus. Some of the conspiracies you hear about are true, but you could be so wrapped up in those speculations that all you think about is how big the devil is. When I talk about these things, it is to point people to the Bible and Jesus, not to bring fear and panic. I am trying to get people to a place where they don't have to panic. I am looking at life with a victory focus, not a defeating focus, and at a place where I can stay in that smooth spot where "I literally abide in him. Then I am invincible."

In God you are indestructible

Have you ever seen Transformers movies? They show some robots where people can actually step in and get into the robot. They are making technology like that now where you literally can climb into a robot, and you move like a bobcat or a bulldozer. In something like that you would be indestructible. But how much more inside God? So, the wisdom is to learn how to stay in the presence of God, learning to abide in Him, making Him my all in all, my priority. Not going back and forth between coming in and coming out. No, just making up my mind that I am going all the way in. I am staying in His presence, and I am not going ankle-deep or waist deep. I am going in and over my head. Hallelujah. To be a part of the last days' army, this is how we will have to be.

One of the things the Lord told me was to raise up an army that would not bow. When pressure comes, I am not bowing. You are going to have to arrest me, you have to burn me at the stake, you have to put a gun to my head. I am not going to deny Christ. I am too much on the other side, and I have gone too far to deny Him now. The key to walking in this place is to heat up your relationship with Him at home.

When you first wake up, learn to train yourself to make God your first priority. Make Him your first focus of the day. Get in the Word and let it become your delight. Let it become your desire. That is what fasting and prayer do. It removes you from food to make the Lord your delight. I am not telling you to be driven and feel like you have to do a forty-day fast and pray for six hours. No, it should be a delight to do it. When my wife and I first met, she said "Do you want to go to a restaurant?" I would say, "Sure, whatever one you want to go to." I got like two hours of sleep, but it was a delight. I do not tell her, "I have an hour and that's it. I gotta go."

Imagine me being with my wife, and I'm on the phone the whole time just looking and scrolling, and she is there. That is not a delight. That is religion. Years ago, when I went to Tampa to be at Pastor Rodney Howard Browne's church, I went there because I wanted more of Jesus. I am here today in Baltimore County not because of obligation but because of relationship. I came because I wanted to follow Him where He was leading me. I just want to be more in His presence. He is better than anything that the world could offer. Listen to me. Even if I wasn't pastoring, I would not want to be anywhere else except the house of the Lord.

David said "...I would rather be a gatekeeper in the house of my God than live the good life in the homes of the wicked." *Psalm 84:10 (NLT)*

He discovered something. David said in *Psalm 27:4-5 (NKJV)*, "One thing I have desired of the Lord, That will I seek: That I may dwell in the house of the Lord All the days of my life, To behold the beauty of the Lord, And to inquire in His temple. For in the time of trouble, He shall hide me in His pavilion". David said one thing he desired was to get under the covering of God and be hidden under His pavilion. That is why when circumstances happen to other people, it does not have to affect you. People see high gas prices and panic, but you can just offer to pay for their gas. It will not affect you if you are under His shelter.

You have got to get that victory in your mind. A thousand will fall by my side; ten thousand at my right hand, but it will not come near me. I am indestructible in the secret place. I am a spectator only, not a participator in the destruction and chaos of the world. As you continue to dwell in the secret place, you will see the hand of the Lord move on your behalf.

I am contending for every person to remain in the secret place. Do not let the devil pull you out of the it. Many great men and women have been pulled out, and now they are back in the ocean of the world because they did not make Jesus their all- in- all. They got distracted. They got pulled out of the presence. Going lukewarm or going cold, it does not just suddenly happen. It is a progression. Think about it. *Song of Solomon 2:15 (NKJV)* says "...The little foxes that spoil the vines." Also, *1 Corinthians 5:6 (KJV)* says: "Know ye not that a little leaven leaveneth the whole lump?".

You must look into your life and say, "Lord, what is in my life that is causing it to be spoiled? What's spoiling the grapes?" A little fox can destroy the vine. A tiny, little fox can take all the grapes from your field. John 15 talks about Jesus being the vine. You are the branches, and He talks about pruning the branches. He prunes so you can continue to bear not only more fruit, but also better fruit. We have all had areas in our lives that needed to be pruned. There may be things that you need to get rid of. There are perhaps certain relationships or objects. Anything in your life that holds you back, you must get rid of. Why? Because it is causing you to go further out of the Kingdom. Those things must go so they do not keep you from being in His presence.

Get wrapped up

If I ever meet a Christian who is distraught and overwhelmed, I ask that person, "When's the last time you've been in God's presence?" Some may say, "Well, I read my Bible a little bit the other day."

That is great, but when was the last time you have been on your face at your house? You know, that place where God takes your breath away. The place where you just sit in your car in a parking lot, turn the music on, and get wrapped up in His presence. Your neighbors may think you are nuts, but who cares? That is where victory comes from, when I am sold out. I love that old gospel song

I am souled out.

My mind is made up.

I am souled out.[1]

---

[1] Souled out by Hezekiah Walker

I am provoking you to get back to where the cares of this world fade away and concerns disappear. If you do not know how things are going to work, get to the secret place. He will speak to you. You might be fearful because you have enemies. Get in the secret place. He will protect you. That is the promise. There is protection in the Most High God. It is not that there are not any challenges, but there is protection.

Psalm 91:4 (AMPC) "[Then] He will cover you with His pinions, and under His wings shall you trust and find refuge; His truth and His faithfulness are a shield and a buckler."

#3: God will answer you.

"...He shall call upon Me, and I will answer him..." *Psalm 91:15 (AMPC)*

The Bible says when you call upon Him, He will answer you. That means He will respond. He will speak to you in the secret place. You may not know what to do. You may be in a crisis with no hope. Get into the secret place. God will tell you in which direction you should go. Then when you ask a leader for counsel, the leader just confirms whatever the Lord already told you. Once you obey what He tells you, then He can give you more instructions. I think about my kids. I will tell them to clean up their rooms, and then we will do something. They come to me and ask if we can get some ice cream. I will say, "What did I tell you?" If they do what I tell them, then they can do the next things.

God is your compass

God says go to that place and then I will answer you. You might ask who to marry, what is the next business decision, or how do I get free from this sin? Get into that place where you abide in God and His Word, so you can get the answer. *John 15:7 (NKJV)* says:" If you abide in Me, and My words abide in you, you will ask what you desire, and it shall be done for you." Do you realize that? That is the place of abiding. That is the place of fully giving your all to God, and then God says I will protect you, I will deliver you, and I will answer you.

I did not have a man tell me to come to Baltimore. My Pastor just confirmed that I was supposed to come. The Lord had already spoken to me in a vision. God spoke to my wife. God spoke to me in the secret place. I knew during COVID that I was going to be all right because I followed what He said to me, and He never fails. I always go back to what He said in the secret place.

#4 God will be with you in trouble

"...I will be with them in trouble." *Psalm 91:15 (AMPC)*

The Bible promises us His presence in times of trouble. You might be worried because of some trouble you are going through, but God said He will be with you. You could be in the worst kind of trouble, but God will bring you out of it. There is a young gentleman named Ryan who works in our ministry who was going to face thirty years in prison. He called on the Lord, and God turned his life around. There is no situation that God cannot change. If you are in trouble, God will bring you out of it when you are in Him.

Psalm 27:1-3 (NKJV) states: "The LORD is my light and my salvation; Whom shall I fear? The LORD is the strength of my life; Of whom shall I be afraid? When the wicked came against me To eat up my flesh, My enemies and foes, They stumbled and fell. Though an army may encamp against me, My heart shall not fear; Though war may rise against me, In this I will be confident."

#5: God will deliver you.

"Because he has set his love upon Me, therefore will I deliver him…" *Psalm 91:14 (AMPC)*

God promises His deliverance. *Psalm 34:4 (NKJV)* says:" I sought the Lord, and He heard me, and delivered me from all my fears."

Any fear we have can be dealt with in the secret place. When you are in a place of protection, there is no need to fear. Fear cannot stay in God's presence. Deliverance comes in the secret place. There is no circumstance He can't deliver you from. No plot of man is too big for Him. When you abide in Him, He hears your cries. This scripture states in *Psalm 107:6: (NKJV)* "Then they cried unto the Lord in their trouble, and he delivered them out of their distresses."

God is a deliverer. The promise of deliverance is given several times in this Psalm. It is given in verses 1, 14, and again in verse 15. It is one thing when God says something once or twice, but three times shows a huge emphasis. God wants us to know this. This is also shown by the number of times God fulfills this promise in scripture. Repeatedly, He delivered Israel. They had troubles with diseases, foreign nations attacking them, severe lack, and more. Many times, those problems were even the results of their own choices, but when they repented and called out, He would still help them.

We see one example of this in Numbers 21. Israel complained and as a result, God allowed serpents in the wilderness to attack them. Previously under His covering, they had been protected from these creatures, but now they, through their own doing, were made vulnerable.

Once they cried out to the Lord, God told Moses to make a pole with a serpent on it. When Israel looked at it, they would be healed. The serpent on the pole is a type and shadow of Jesus' becoming sin for us. As we look to Him and what He did when He was lifted up on the cross, we can be healed.

If He would help them under the old covenant, how much more will He help you under the new one?

If He would deliver his people even when they had been rebellious and stubborn, how much more will He help you if you abide in Him?

#6: God will honor you

"...and honor him." *Psalm 91:15 (AMPC)*

This scripture promises that He will honor you. Honor comes from the secret place. That is why He said when you go and pray, do not be like the Pharisees and the Sadducees. Do not be like the scribes. They only want to be seen in public. They only want to be seen on a microphone at church, but back home they are living like devils. They have pitchforks. They are gossiping about everybody in the church. They are saying, "I'm righteous. I do more than that person, so I don't know why that person got promoted tonight." When they are back in church, they smile and praise the Lord.

Private devotion brings open reward

Go to a place away from everybody else and seek after God. Just draw close to Him in private, and He says what is done in secret will be rewarded openly. That is the secret place. It is the place where you do not need anybody to tell you to lift your hands. Nobody to tell you to open your Bible. I have decided to live in that place. When I am off work or out of church, I have free time. I have decided I am going to spend more of that time in the secret place. I am spending it where it is the Lord and me. He told the church in Ephesus to come back to their first love. (See *Revelation 2:4*) Come back, not to religion, but to their first love, to the place where the number one thing they wanted is Him.

I remember when I first got saved. I would take my phone, and I would throw it on my bed and just go out in the woods. I had a guitar. I could not play it worth anything, so I just strummed it, looked up at the stars, and sang random songs to the Lord. I am telling you the presence of God would come and just hit me as I did that. I would lie on the hammock outside and listen to worship music. When I first got saved, I felt very strongly that I was to spend time with Him in worship. I did not even know all that much about God at that time. All I knew is that Jesus was my Lord, and I wanted more of Him. I would spend time with Him until I was lost in His presence. I am not just talking about attending church. I am talking about intimacy with my Father. As I came to know Him more, He would speak to me. He would give me dreams. I would spend time with God and then go to my job where I was working at a construction site. I would carry a ladder, just smile, and say hi to everyone. They wanted to know what was wrong with me, but I didn't even know what I was doing differently. I was in the secret place. I would get promoted in my job, and things were working out supernaturally. I was on fire and people could see it. That is the place where God wants you to remain. Not ups and downs. Not defeats. A place where God can speak to you, and you can hear him clearly. A place of total protection. A place where God promises to remove anything that opposes you. God promises to honor you in that place with Him.

#7: God will satisfy you with long life.

"With long life will I satisfy him…" *Psalm 91:16 (AMPC)*

In the secret place, your life can be long. Many say:" You never know when your time will be up." No, the scripture shows that you can live a long life.

Others say, "Well, you don't know when the Lord will pluck you to be a flower in His garden."

This is wrong thinking because the truth of the Bible states the opposite. It says: "Honor your father and your mother, that your days may be long upon the land which the LORD your God is giving you." *Exodus 20:12 (NKJV)*. The devil cannot kill me because I honor my father and mother and I dwell in the secret place. He said, "...with long life I will satisfy him." *Psalm 91:16 (NKJV)*.

You can live a long life. Maybe someone told you that you would die early. Don't listen to that lie! Get into the secret place. The devil cannot kill you there. When your time is up, then you will go and not before.

I had someone talk to me one night, and he told me that being sixty meant he was going to die. I said, "You're sixty. Come on, you have at least twenty years in you. Sixty is not old." Some people in this season of their lives decide to just retire and play Bingo. You need to get out and get moving because God is not finished with you. God gives long life, and God still has great purpose for you.

God promises you long life in the secret place.

#8: God will show you His salvation.

"...And show him my salvation." *Psalm 91:16 (AMPC)*

The definition of salvation has many facets. In Greek, it is the word *Sozo*. In this language, it means deliverance, healing, and breakthrough. It is an all-inclusive word. In Psalm 91 when you look at salvation in Hebrew the word is *Yeshua*. This makes sense because He is our deliverance.

God wants to save in every area of our lives. He did not just die for one area. He did not take just one part of the curse. Some say we are only healed spiritually, but that contradicts the very life Jesus lived. The Book of Acts says: "...how God anointed Jesus of Nazareth with the Holy Spirit and with power, who went about doing good and healing all who were oppressed by the devil, for God was with Him." *Acts 10:38 (NKJV)*

Was Jesus only healing people spiritually? No, the healing was both natural and spiritual. He even fed people supernaturally with food by multiplying it. Jesus didn't leave and then suddenly become concerned only with our spirit. Salvation is for every area. We are delivered from the curse, not just some of it.

To end this chapter, let us go through the list again.

#1: I will rescue him and deliver him from every disease.

#2: I will protect him.

#3: I will answer him.

#4: I will be with him in trouble.

#5: I will deliver him.

#6: I will honor him.

#7: I will satisfy him with long life.

#8: I will show him My salvation.

These promises are available to all. It is time to get into the secret place, and then you can claim these promises for your life.

CHAPTER 6

Are You in the Shadow?

I remember back in the day when my brother and I used to play NBA Jam. It is a funny, old Nintendo game. If you made a dunk in the basket, the announcer would say, "Boom! Chakalaka!!" If you made three baskets in a row, the announcer would yell, «HE'S ON FIRE!!» Then your character's ball would be lit up with a flame. At that point, you could throw the ball from anywhere, and it went in regardless. You could throw it backward, and it would go in. It didn't matter. You were invincible when you had the fire.

Do you realize that is what the day of Pentecost was about? It was about a group of people who decided to get under the shadow. You can do the same, but don't just do it once; stay in that place. Every day, come into His presence. That is the place of victory. The devil wants you away from God's presence, so he has access to you.

All the King has is yours

Let's look at Luke chapter 15: the Prodigal Son. One of the sons decides he wants his inheritance now. Then he wastes the money on worthless things and winds up in trouble. Imagine being at church and wanting to get high on some drug. Or maybe feeling the need to go fornicate. Why would someone feel that way? The answer is that they are in church, but they are not in the secret place. The devil wants to make you vulnerable by taking you away from that place. That is what he did to the prodigal son when he tempted him away from his father's protection and began to attack him.

Then you have the other brother who was in religion.

One day the older brother came around and saw the father rejoicing. He wanted to know what all the excitement was about. He heard that his brother was back and as a result, there was a celebration.

Pouting, he goes to his dad and says, "Why are you giving him the robe of honor and putting the ring on his finger? What's going on?"

Then in verse 31, the dad says, ".... All that I have is yours." (NKJV). It was already his. Many have been in the kingdom, but they have not been in the secret place to have access to the things that God already has for them.

Have you ever heard that saying, "If it was a snake, it should have bitten you?" Have you ever been looking for your keys, and they are sitting right there on your dresser? Then your kid finds those keys and shows them to you. They were there on the dresser the whole time. Many times when I was working in construction, I would always ask, "Where's my pencil? They told me that it was on my ear.

I want you to be in that place where you do not have to run back to the world. There is a covering for you that you never have to leave. People often feel a need to run back to the world and get some kind of covering. No, I'm telling you the secret place of the Most High is the only one you need.

Earlier when I talked about the promise in Psalm 91 that a thousand will fall at your side and ten thousand at your right hand, but you will only be a spectator. There is good spectating and bad.

To illustrate, when I was younger, the guys who I worked with were all about football. They loved certain teams, and it did not matter who played; at lunchtime it was football talk. They were like, "I can't believe we lost, and we should have caught that touchdown. We should have caught that pass. We are just too slow." I looked at them and said, "We?" Some of these guys could barely climb a ladder, and they were talking about "we" like they were on the field.

Spectators always know what to do even though they are not doing it. They yell at the TV or directly at the team if at a live game. They yell, "Run!!" or "Man, why did you drop the ball?"

In Psalm 91, it is the good side of spectating. It is saying you will just watch your enemies fall before you. That will be your story in Jesus' name. You will see destruction, not in your own life, but you will watch it as a spectator. Then God says, "I will prepare a table before you in the presence of your enemies in the secret place." When

I am loving God and obeying what He is telling me to do, that is where the secret place is. That is the place where I can't be destroyed. I can't. It is impossible. You cannot be destroyed in that place of obedience and loving God with all your heart, your mind, your soul, and strength.

Make God your refuge

The Bible says in *Psalm 5:11 (AMPC)* "But let all those who take refuge *and* put their trust in You rejoice..." If you make God your refuge, you can be the person who lives your life rejoicing instead of mourning.

You might wonder how anyone can be happy. You might be fearful because they passed this or that law. We should never be worried though because we have angels with us. You don't have to be afraid of anything.

For example, in the month of December, we do a Christmas outreach. On one occasion we went to a very crime-ridden neighborhood called Cherry Hill. It was a phenomenal event where 1600 people came out, and over 1000 people gave their lives to the Lord. Directly after the main message and altar call, a random guy walked up and stood ten feet in front of me and just stared. I knew in my spirit he wanted to kill me. When I looked at him, I asked him if I could help him, but with his eyes glaring at me and his body shaking, I knew he was demon-possessed. I was not going to fight him. Getting into violence was not necessary. I stood my ground in the secret place. He could not touch me. If you abide in God, no one can touch you either.

Do you realize that? Witchcraft can't touch you in the secret place. Famine and disease can't touch you. Even though it can happen around you, it can't affect you. That is where we must be. We must be more secret place-conscious than demon-conscious. We must be more focused on getting into and remaining in God's presence and not worrying about the wicked.

In *Psalm 37:1 (NKJV)* it says, "Do not fret because of evildoers, Nor be envious of the workers of iniquity."

This psalm tells us not to worry about their evil schemes.

We do not have to fear. They can move us all to North Korea, and we will prosper. They can put us in China, and we will still prosper. They tried to do that in the book of Acts. Look at Peter breaking out of prison or at Paul praising His way out. They could not stop the church.

Do not go before your time

Some may say, "Well, Pastor, they crucified Peter, and they beheaded Paul." Yes, but not before their time. When the time was up, they said, "Okay, I am getting out of here." Even Jesus said of his life: "No one takes it from Me, but I lay it down of Myself. I have power to lay it down, and I have power to take it again. This command I have received from My Father." *John 10:18 (NKJV)*. There is a place in God that you can go to where this will be your reality.

CHAPTER 7

In the Building but Not Under the Cover

When you were a kid and you fell from a bike, who did you call? You did not call a friend. No, you called Mama or Daddy, Grandma, or whoever you had in your life. Why? Because when I call my mom, she is going to take care of me. When we abide in God's presence, He can be the one we run to for taking care of us. Many things deter people, but a big one is pride. To operate in the secret place, there must be a spirit of humility. It takes humility to come under a covering. It really does. The world does not want to be under any covering. If you look at the rappers or the rock stars, they become their own gods. You can even hear it in their songs. Their songs are about them being their own god. It is all about them. It is not about Him. The world does not want to be under the covering of God.

Keep your lamp filled

In Matthew, Jesus talked about people who were covered and people who were not covered in the church. Earlier I talked about a parable in Matthew 22 with three disobedient servants. In another parable, He talks about people who had oil and people who did not have oil - the five wise and five foolish virgins. The foolish ones were in the church but not in the covering of the church. Not everyone who goes to church is going to make it in the rapture.

Let me say it again. Not everyone inside the church is going to make it when the trumpet blows, only those who are in the covering. Only those who are in Christ. It is not just coming to church and saying a prayer, and then going back to doing whatever. No, it is not that. It is a life of repentance. It is a life of abiding and giving up your life. If you try to gain your life, you will lose it, but if you lose your life for His sake, you will find it (*see Matthew 10:39*).

That is the kingdom. That is how the kingdom operates. You might think you do not want to give God your all because then it will just be a boring life. You will never live a boring life with the King. We have the uncreated Creator who created all these things that the Discovery channel is still trying to figure out. They still have not discovered even half the ocean, let alone space. But God made it all, and He wants a relationship with you and me.

God wants to meet with you

Everybody wants to talk to my Pastor, Rodney Howard Browne. When he gets finished preaching, people eagerly desire to get his attention and speak with him. People want to get to know Pastor Rodney, and there is nothing wrong with that. He is a great and anointed man of God, but I thought about this. Is everybody like that with the Lord?

Some just want to meet Pastor or Apostle so and so. They hope maybe he will take them into his office. They dream of going out to eat together one day and that is great. Yes, you can get to know them, but I want you to get to know Jesus because He is the one who is going to be with you at four in the morning. He is going to be the one who tells you the right way to go. Perhaps I could tell you human wisdom. Maybe I could get something from God, but this is not (and God bless all the Catholics) Catholicism. I don't cut a hole in my wall and sit there and say, "What have you done today?" while someone confesses all their sins. I don't tell people to hail Mary five times. None of that. I am not building the relationship between you and me. I am trying to build it between you and Him. He is the one who is your refuge. He is the one. Yes, I can cover you in prayer. Yes, I can lay my hands on you. Yes, I can operate in the gifts and all that, but the greatest covering is to be covered by Him because He is the one who is covering me. If He is covering me, I will just point you to Him. Yes, I have a Pastor who prays for and covers me, but my covering is really being with the Lord in His presence. There is a place of ultimate victory called the secret place, and it is for you.

CHAPTER 8

The Promises Are Not Automatic

Some people quote scriptures, but they do not see the condition in the scripture. There are always conditions in anything. In your car, there are conditions and restrictions. There are things that you do, and you do not do. For instance, you do not put diesel fuel in a gasoline car.

Certain actions unlock scriptures. For example, how do you get saved? Well, there is something that you must do. *Romans 10:9 (NKJV)* says: "that if you confess with your mouth the Lord Jesus and believe in your heart that God has raised Him from the dead, you will be saved." If you don't do that, you are not saved. You have to stay in a relationship with Jesus, continue walking with Him, and live a repentant life. The Bible says: "But he that shall endure unto the end, the same shall be saved." *Matthew 24:13 (KJV)*. There is a condition for salvation just like there is a condition for healing. You say what is the condition? The Bible says: "Is anyone among you sick? Let him call for the elders of the church, and let them pray over him, anointing him with oil in the name of the Lord. And the prayer of faith will save the sick, and the Lord will raise him up. And if he has committed sins, he will be forgiven." *James 5:14-16 (NKJV).* Getting anointed with oil and receiving the prayer of faith is a condition for healing.

Obedience unlocks the promises

This is also true when it comes to finances. Prosperity is a blessing that God has made available for His children. If we want to walk in this, then tithing and giving is the key. Scripture tells us to bring all the tithes into the storehouse (Malachi 3:10). If we obey God's Word, it promises that God will:

"...open for you the windows of heaven
And pour out for you such blessing
That *there will* not be room enough to *receive* it."
Malachi 3:10 (NKJV)

Conditions are a part of every promise. We may want angels, protection, or any other blessing God has, but there must be a willingness to do what scripture says. James says: "But be doers of the word, and not hearers only, deceiving yourselves." *James 1:22 (NKJV)*

The promises in Psalm 91 are no different. Each has an action that unlocks them. The conditions for Psalm 91 are in these few scriptures: Psalm 91 verses 1, 9 and 14. *(AMPC)*

Let's examine these verses. Verse 1 *(AMPC)* says, "He who dwells in the secret place." That's the condition. To dwell means to live or abide in His presence. God is not interested in dating or courting but in being married. My wife and I are in covenant. I do not want anyone else except her. I'm done. I have seen that my wife is good. In fact, she is so good that I am done with other women. I do not want anyone else. I have made up my mind that she and I are together till death do us part. We are abiding with each other. Come hell or high water. No matter what, it is her and me. Now even with us being in covenant, I must keep the flavor in the marriage. I have to keep intimacy between us. I have to take my wife out on dates. I have to tell her that I love her. We must spend time together. When she is talking to me, I can't be saying, "Look, I'm busy right now." No, I must give her my attention and show that she is important to me. I need to listen and be attentive to her needs and wants. Yet as much as you need to love your spouse, if you want a marriage to flow correctly, you must love God more than you love that spouse.

It is the same with your kids. If you want your kids to serve God, you have got to love God more than you love those kids. Some parents love their kids more than they love God, and that is why the kids are so rebellious. God teaches that if you love them, then you are going to correct them. You are going to give them discipline because God says to do so. Some parents say, "Well, I love them, so I will never spank them." You need to spank them because God loves you, and you love and trust Him. Trusting God means accepting His Word over anyone else's opinion on the subject.

Verse 9 (*AMPC*) speaks of making the Lord your refuge. Making Him your refuge is keeping Him in first place. It is knowing He is your source of protection, not the world. God wants to be your shelter in the storm and stronghold in trouble.

There are many places people run to for help, but God says you can make Him your place of refuge if you make Him first in your life.

Finally, verse 14 (*AMPC*) says this: "Because he set his love upon Me..." Look at that. If we set our love on Him, He will deliver us. The more you fall in love with God, the greater your life becomes. Every man of God in scripture experienced this. David was a nobody, and God took him out and made him a somebody.

Staying in the shelter

We must walk in these promises in the last days because there are people with an evil agenda that opposes God.

They are bent on destroying lives and instituting a world under their control. To do this their number one goal is the collapse of the whole governance of America and ultimately the world. There is a plan to reset the world. It is a fact. They meet literally every year at a place in Davos, Switzerland, and they discuss how to shut down the world to re-govern it. These goals are not even hidden anymore. There are high official government leaders who are satanists and want to destroy the earth as we know it. Many people now think Covid is all over, so they will just go back to life as normal. The problem with that is these people who planned Covid are going to hit that button again. I am telling you right now, it is just a matter of when they are going to hit it. They are going to create something else. There are plans to kill people. I am not a conspiracy theorist. I think you can get way too caught up listening to conspiracy "experts." This, however, does not mean there are not real things happening. You do not have to go to conspiracy theorists to hear these views. The people planning these things admit it publicly. Bill Gates said, "If we do a really good job on new vaccines, health care, reproductive services, we could lower that (referring to the population) by perhaps 10 or 15 percent."[2]

That is why they tried to push the vaccines everywhere. There are things like this happening because we live in the last days. Jesus said there will be famines. There will be pestilence. There will be earthquakes. There will be all these things, and He talks about the times and the seasons. (See *Matthew 24:7*) You will see it. Jesus is coming back soon, but before then there will be chaos. Yet in the secret place you will be covered.

No time to waste

In addition to the promises of Psalm 91, I will give some additional promises from His Word before I end this chapter.

Psalm 31:19-20 states in the *NKJV:*

"Oh, how great is Your goodness,
Which You have laid up for those who fear You,
Which You have prepared for those who trust in You
In the presence of the sons of men!

---

[2] Bill Gates 2010 Ted Talk "Innovating to 0"

You shall hide them in the secret place of Your presence
From the plots of man;
You shall keep them secretly in a pavilion.
From the strife of tongues."

Then in *Psalm 5:11-12 (AMPC)*, it says: "But let all those who take refuge and put their trust in you rejoice; let them ever sing and shout for joy, because you make a covering over them and defend them; let those also who love Your name be joyful in You and be in high spirits."

There has to be results

We are near the end of time. We do not have the luxury of wasting the days we have left with fruitless pursuits. One thing I know is if I am going to invest in something, I must get results from it. If not, I will do something else. I do not want to play teacups with God. Have you ever played teacups? My kids will say they have a donut for me, but it is a plastic donut and I pretend to eat it. Then they bring out empty cups that I will pretend to drink tea from, and I tell them how good it is.

Do you want to be a Christian who plays teacups with God, or do you want the Bible to work? You have got to be a doer of the Word. Dwelling in Him is the condition for walking in His promises. I can't emphasize that point enough. God wants to be married to you, not date you. That is the condition for accessing these promises. Suppose you were dating someone, and you asked that person to commit to marriage, but your proposal was refused. This person wanted to see other people and therefore would not be given any of the protection, provision, and benefits of a spouse by you. Likewise, we cannot date God and expect His covenant promises in our lives. God loves you, wants to be with you, and wants to cover you. In the next chapter, I will show that this covering is greater than any other.

CHAPTER 9

Who is More Powerful?

$n$ot that long ago something happened that made Papa Bear come out blazing. My daughter had a birthday, and we went to a skating rink to celebrate. She started skating and got halfway around the rink. At that point two kids, who were around thirteen or fourteen-years old, kicked her in the back of the skates, and she hit the ground hard. When I first got to the skating rink, I was very nice. But when my daughter got hurt, I became like an evangelist dealing with a demon at a tent revival. Something just switched.

I was being nice. I was being a good pastor, but I heard my baby crying.

I asked her what was going on. She said that some boys pushed her. Instantly, my whole tone changed, and I asked her what color clothes the boys were wearing so I could find them.

Some guy came up to me and said that he saw my daughter get pushed. Immediately I asked him to show me who it was. This was my girl's birthday, and she was crying, so I wanted to know who did it. Once I found out, I was very serious when I told them to come over to me. See, they did not know that Dad was in the house. Now I did not do anything; I wanted to, but I did not. However, my eyes of fire touched their souls as I spoke to them, and my baby was behind me like, "Yeah, Dad, get 'em."

These boys did not know that someone was backing and covering her. The moment she cried to me, the moment she came closer to me, suddenly I covered her even more. When she got hurt, I went into war mode. Why? Because I was covering my daughter. If she had not invited me to her birthday party, I could not have covered her. If she distanced herself from me, how could I have covered her as a father?

The place of constant victory

You need to say, "God, I want you with me everywhere I go." When you live that way, if something is wrong, you just praise Him and let Him step in. And not only does God step in the way, but the Word also says, "For He will give His angels [especial] charge over you to accompany and defend and preserve you in all your ways [of obedience and service]." *Psalm 91:11 (AMPC)*

Some people get worried about witches. My question is, who is more powerful? An angel of the Lord or a witch? The Holy Spirit is inside of you. You have God living on the inside of you. You do not have to look up. You just look down at your belly. Say "Holy Spirit, I know you are living inside of me and greater is He that is in me." With you in

Him and He in you, your life only goes forward, and nothing can destroy you.

There needs to be a covering. That is why you live in a house. You need a covering. That is why you come to a church and submit under a house of God. It is so you can be protected. A covering is very powerful.

I saw something once on a show that was a good illustration of what I am talking about. It was about forty degrees outside, and a man had a convertible with the whole top down, going seventy miles an hour. If it snowed or rained, he would be freezing. There was no covering. That is what it is like going through life, but not living under God's protection.

I am endeavoring to show you how to stay in the covering of God. Coming to church is great, but it is not everything. Some people come to church all the time, but they still struggle. You talk to them, and they talk about all the things the devil is doing in their life. You ask them what they are doing because the Bible is a book of victory, not a book of defeat. Let me say it again. The Bible is a book of victory. If you are constantly being defeated, then something is wrong. Some people say, "Well, you know, you win some; you lose some. Blessed be the name of the Lord." But that is not in the Bible.

When David wrote his psalms, he would talk about the bad things that were going on, but just keep reading. He says in *Psalm 121:1 (NKJV)*" I will lift up my eyes to the hills -- from whence comes my help?" David did not deny challenges, but he knew where his help came from.

God will make you strong in the Secret Place

Some go to a gym to get strong physically, but God's presence is where we go to be strengthened spiritually. That supernatural strength will cause us to be able to do great exploits for God. The Secret Place is where God's giants are made. Let's look at *Isaiah 40:26 (NKJV):*

"Lift up your eyes on high, And see who has created these *things,* Who brings out their host by number; He calls them all by name, By the greatness of His might And the strength of *His* power; Not one is missing. Why do you say, O Jacob, And speak, O Israel: "My way is hidden from the Lord, And my just claim is passed over by my God?" Have you not known? Have you not heard? The everlasting God, the Lord, The Creator of the ends of the earth, Neither faints nor is weary His understanding is unsearchable. He gives power to the weak, And to *those who have* no might He increases strength. Even the youths shall faint and be weary, And the young men shall utterly fall, But those who wait on the Lord Shall renew *their* strength; They shall mount up with wings like eagles, They shall run and not be weary, They shall walk and not faint."

We are meant to be a mighty army in His strength. If we are not abiding in God we end up living in our own strength and that can cause us to be taken out by the enemy. In the days ahead especially we have to live in the strength of God not the arm of the flesh.

His arm is not short

There is no challenge that you are facing that God cannot do something about or empower you to overcome. There is nothing too hard for the Lord. We do not serve a God who has short hands. God has a strong arm. That strong arm picked David out of the pit and made him king. Why? David was in the secret place. David decided that he just wanted Jesus. He decided to make God his all in all. He decided God would be his permanent dwelling place. Some people only go to church when all hell breaks loose, and I get it. I did that. But then I started getting more in the church. I decided to stop going back and forth. Jesus is not a crisis ATM. He's not a credit card that you swipe when you do not have anything else. No, He must be first place. He must be a dwelling place, a place where He is your number one. In the Old Testament, the first commandment says, "Don't have any idols before me." (See *Exodus 20:3*) God says He is a jealous God. Some may have a hard time with that, but God is Jehovah Jealous. Imagine you are walking home, and your spouse is talking to somebody else on a romantic level. You would get jealous. You think it is just you and your spouse, but there is someone else. Do you realize that you are the bride, and He is the groom? When the bride makes Him number one and gets ready for that engagement, He says, "Okay, I will cover you now."

Get rid of the idols

You might think you don't have idols because there is not some big Baal statue in your life, but an idol is anything you love more than God. Religion occurs when spending time with Him is a chore.

Once again, using marriage as an example, I do not look at my wife and think, "I have to take you out to dinner." I don't choose the cheapest option and watch the time all evening. God does not want that kind of relationship either. As you spend time with God and prioritize Him, He will meet with you. Spending time will not just be a chore. That is how you return to your first love; you prioritize Him like you did when you first got saved.

CHAPTER 10

God Wants You More Than You Want Him

*I*ntimacy is what God wants. That is the theme of this entire book. This is the supreme dinner bell of everything. This is 1 Kings 3. When Solomon loved the Lord with all his heart, he offered a thousand burnt rams. Then God went to Solomon and said to him,"What do you want?" Solomon answered that he wanted wisdom to help God's people. He just wanted God's heart, but God decided to give him everything else.

Solomon did not do it out of religion; he did it out of intimacy. Fasting should not be because of religion. We are not supposed to come to church because of religion. We are supposed to come because we want to come. When we love God, we do not need someone asking, "Did you read your Bible?" God's Word is like honey to me. In fact, it is sweeter than honey. It is better than any relationship. It is better than any Taco Tuesday, and I like Taco Tuesday. His Word is greater than anything. The Bible is the book of victory. It is life to those who find them and health to all their flesh. (See *Proverbs 4:22 NKJV*) It is a double-edged sword. This is the Word. God wants us to love the Word more than we love our favorite food. We can know the uncreated

Creator. When I discover the mountains, animals, and trees, I am in awe. I am amazed when I look at these things and realize this God who made them wants to live on the inside of me. He wants to know you and me. He wants to love us. Why wouldn't I want a relationship with the Most High God? When He says knock and I will answer, He is knocking on the door of your heart because He wants to be with you. He numbers the hairs on your head. No bird falls to the ground without His knowing it. But forget the birds; He wants you. That is what God is saying. For God so loved the world, not the trees, the birds, the bees. He loves you, and all He says is come.

As I talked about earlier, Jesus cried to Israel: "Oh, Jerusalem... how often I wanted to gather your children together, as a hen gathers her chicks under her wings, but you were not willing." He wanted to protect them, but they refused. (See *Matthew 23:37 NKJV*). But that is not going to be me, and I believe it will not be the people reading this. Let us all cry, "Lord, let me go further." It is time to go into the depths of the water, shut down distractions, and get lost in Him. We must just get back to our first works, to the first love. See, we need to return to the time when we first came to Christ.

Nothing matters more than Him

When we fall in love with Jesus, nothing else compares to Him. I did not need drugs anymore. I had to separate myself from previous relationships that tried to offer me things I should never have been into. Nothing was greater than Jesus. I have been high on some bad things. I am not proud of that, but I have been high. There is no high like the Most High. That is why the Bible says, "And be not drunk with wine, wherein is excess; but be filled with the Spirit." *Ephesians 5:18(KJV)*. You do not need the covering of wine. That is why the Bible says in *Psalm 34:8 (KJV)*: "O taste and see that the Lord is good…" I dare you to take this week and do something differently. Delete some apps on your phone. Some folks are on their phone eight hours a day, looking at other people's lives. It is time to lay that down and live your life with the King. I am not telling you that you can't have fun, but you have to have God above everything.

God is a God of secrets

Even though God wants to be known by His children, He is not what some would call an easy catch. He must be diligently pursued. God's secrets are priceless, and He doesn't just reveal them to everyone. Being close to His heart is the greatest privilege. He hides from the proud and those who are too full of other things to thirst after Him. We must be determined if we are going after God. This pursuit comes with great rewards, and the Bible says it in several verses:

Psalms 25:14-15 (KJV)
"The secret of the LORD is with them that fear him; And he will shew them his covenant. Mine eyes are ever toward the LORD; For he shall pluck my feet out of the net."

Isaiah 45:15 (NKJV)

"Truly You are God, who hide Yourself,
O God of Israel, the Savior!"

Proverbs 25:2 (NKJV)

"It is the glory of God to conceal a matter,
But the glory of kings is to search out a matter."

Deuteronomy 29:29 (NKJV)

"The secret *things belong* to the Lord our God,
but those *things which are* revealed *belong to*
us and to our children forever, that *we* may do all
the words of this law."

Mark 4:10-11 (NKJV)

"But when He was alone, those around Him with
the twelve asked Him about the parable. And He
said to them, "To you it has been given to know
the mystery of the kingdom of God; but to those
who are outside, all things come in parables,
so that 'Seeing they may see and not perceive,
And hearing they may hear and not understand;
Lest they should turn, And *their* sins be forgiven
them.'"

God wants to reveal Himself and His heart to you.
In our lives all of us have things we eagerly went after. It is
time to put that passion and determination into our pursuit
of Him.

There is a place...

CHAPTER 11

Crazy to People but Normal to God

*L*ook at the life of John the Baptist. John the Baptist was eating honey and locusts in the wilderness. His hair was wrecked, and he just wore a camel skin held together with a belt. I used to think he was weird, but I don't anymore. John was in the secret place. He was not affected by city life; he did not need all that. He was having intimacy with the King. Did you know John probably had some crazy encounters? He probably was so wrapped in the glory of God that he didn't want to go back. He lived out in the wilderness by himself and just preached because what he was experiencing was heaven on earth. He was experiencing what he was created to do.

Your real purpose

You were created not to play golf or football or fix cars or whatever your occupation is. That might be a part of what you do, but do you know what you were really called to do? You are called to worship the King. Your hands were not hands made primarily to play games. No, your hands and my hands were made to worship. Our mouths were not made just to communicate. They were made to praise. Our eyes were not made just to see natural things. No, they were designed to see the glory of God, and therefore our bodies were designed to respond to what we see. Our knees were made to kneel before the Lord. As you continue in your first love, you are fulfilling your original purpose, which is to be intimate with the King.

God just wants you to love Him

This is a love relationship not just a religion. God wants people who will love Him in response to how He has loved them. The greatest thing a parent desires, who truly loves each child, is for each child to return that love. God is no different. Whatever my kids are called to do, whatever God wants for them, all I want is for them to love on me. When I came home from Tampa one time and I opened the door, I was surprised with gifts everywhere. My children had Reese's Pieces and gifts they made for me, and they all showered me with kisses and hugs. I could care less about the candy. Sometimes that is all parents want. They just want their kids to lay the toys down and love them. When they do that with me, I open up. I tell them we can do whatever they want. But when they get rebellious, and they are fighting, bickering, and talking about each other, that is different. People say they want the blessing, but they are fighting with people in the church. There are arguments and quarrels and conflict. That is when God sends you to timeout.

We are not doing this for the blessing. We are doing this because we appreciate what He has done for us. Many should be dead or in an insane asylum right now. I should be in hell where there is no water, no food, and barely any oxygen with demons torturing me day and night. Hell is a place of constant harassment with no protection from God, and no peace forever. Yet God came and saved me. Do you know how much I owe this to the Lord? Listen, even if He never did anything else for me, that is enough for me to worship Him. That is enough for me to say, "God, I'm thankful."

I am just giving Him thanks every day for all that He already has done in my life. The Lord has given me a beautiful wife, a family, and much more. God has given me everything.

How did I even end up in this position? I don't know. Sometimes I ask myself, "Am I really a pastor?" I was a drug addict and a nut job. I had demons inside of me. I had voices telling me to kill myself. Now I stand here clothed in my right mind. I'm so grateful. The Lord crossed land and sea to get you out of the hell that you were in also. Now He is reminding you to get back into that place with Him. Get into that refuge and fortress. If you are dabbling outside of that tent, you better get back inside. There is nothing good on the outside. Referencing back to the prodigal son, he learned it the hard way. He got his money, and he went out into the world. Then he started eating with pigs and said, "Man, this stinks. I'm going back to the king." He ran back to his Father. And guess what? God restored him.

Maybe you have never grasped that God is your Father and that is what has kept you from drawing near to Him. Maybe you think God just wants to punish and condemn, but that is not the truth. Once you are in the kingdom, you have a new Father. That might be tough to grasp because perhaps you did not have a father when you were growing up. Or maybe something you read had a father, but not a good one. God is your Father, and He is perfect. The Lord has always watched over you. He has adopted you. You might ask, "What does He want from me?" He wants your heart. It is easy serving God. It is not hard. It is hard serving the devil. Jesus said, "For My yoke is easy, and My burden is light." (*Matthew 11:30 KJV*)

You need to know that He is not a condemning judge waiting for you to come. God does judge, but if you come with a heart that says, "God, I just want to know you; I don't want to be outside anymore," He will welcome you in with no condemnation.

Let this be the day you decide to go back to Him, and then you will go into realms in which you have never been.

Break up your schedule. Maybe go to bed later or get up earlier. God will make up that time as you spend it with Him. Your favorite show can wait. Your favorite activity can wait. Make God your favorite.

Don't wait until later

The Bible says: "Repent therefore and be converted, that your sins may be blotted out, so that times of refreshing may come from the presence of the Lord," *Acts 3:19 (NKJV)*.

If you are not where you should be with God, it is time to make a change. God is drawing, He is wooing His people to come back to that place, not just clapping their hands or hearing a three-point sermon and going back into being distracted. No, it is a time to be intimate with God. What if the trumpet blew and you were not in Christ?

We must get real with God now because there will be a point where there is not a second chance. I am inviting you to the place where you will overcome. This is the place you are going to get direction. This is where you are going to find fulfillment, peace, and victory. It is where your life will be guided by Him and in the end, you will hear, "Well done, good and faithful servant." (See *Matthew 25:23*)

CHAPTER 12

How to Seek God's Presence

I have included some practical and scriptural steps to help you seek after the Lord. Let these be a guide to help you pursue His heart and overcome any obstacles to knowing Him more deeply.

1. Come clean

We must genuinely confess and repent of any known sin that we have committed. Do not try to justify sin. We can never be free of any sins if we make excuses for them. God knows everything, so bring it to Him.

Acts 3:19-20 (AMPC)

"So repent (change your mind and purpose); turn around and return [to God], that your sins may be erased (blotted out, wiped clean), that times of refreshing (of recovering from the effects of heat, of reviving with fresh air) may come from the presence of the Lord; And that He may send [to you] the Christ (the Messiah),

Who before was designated and appointed for you—even Jesus,"

Psalm 32:5 (ESV)

"I acknowledged my sin to you, and I did not cover my iniquity; I said, 'I will confess my transgressions to the Lord,' and you forgave the iniquity of my sin."

1 John 1:9 (ESV)

"If we confess our sins, he is faithful and just and just to forgive us our sins and cleanse us from all unrighteousness."

Proverbs 28:13 (ESV)

"Whoever conceals his transgressions will not prosper, but he who confesses and forsakes them will obtain mercy."

2. Check your motives

While we can bring our requests to God, the requests and motives behind them have to line up with His Word.

James 4:2-4 (NKJV)

"You lust and do not have. You murder and covet and cannot obtain. You fight and war. Yet you do not have because you do not ask. You ask and do not receive, because you ask amiss, that you may spend it on your pleasures. Adulterers and adulteresses! Do you not know that friendship with the world is enmity with God? Whoever therefore wants to be a friend of the world makes himself an enemy of God."

Proverbs 16:2 (ESV)

"All the ways of a man are pure in his own eyes, but the Lord weighs the spirit."

3. Be real with God

God abhors hypocrisy. Be real, come as you are, and do not try to put up a front with Him. He knows your deepest secrets, so trying to be something you are not is pointless and a hindrance to a deeper relationship. There is no need to be phony with Him.

Matthew 15:8 (ESV)

"This people honors me with their lips, but their heart is far from me".

Matthew 5:8 (ESV)

"Blessed are the pure in heart, for they shall see God."

4. Begin to seek the Lord

Both the Old and New Testaments say to set our minds and hearts on God. We are to consciously set our focus upon Him.

1 Chronicles 22:19 (ESV)

"Now set your mind and heart to seek the Lord your God..."

Colossians 3:1–2 (ESV)

"If then you have been raised with Christ, seek the things that are above, where Christ is, seated at the right hand of God. Set your minds on things that are above, not on things that are on earth. "

Isaiah 55:6 (ESV)

"Seek the Lord while he may be found; call upon him while he is near."

5. Refuse to go by your feelings

Our feelings and emotions are not consistently a good compass for our lives. We must always be led by the Word and the Spirit.

2 Corinthians 5:7 (ESV)

"For we walk by faith, not by sight."

Proverbs 3:5-6 (ESV)

"Trust in the Lord with all your heart, and do not lean on your own understanding. In all your ways acknowledge him, and he will make straight your paths."

6. Be consistent

Like anything worth pursuing, walking with God requires consistency. We won't get far if our pursuit of Him is not steady. The Bible says:" But without faith it is impossible to please Him, for he who comes to God must believe that He is, and *that* He is a rewarder of those who diligently seek Him." *Hebrews 11:6* (NKJV)

2 Thessalonians 3:5 (ESV)
> "May the Lord direct your hearts to the love of God and to the steadfastness of Christ."

Psalms 105:4 (ESV)
> "Seek the Lord and His strength;
> seek His presence continually!"

Prayer

I thank You, Lord, that the people reading this book are going to contend for that secret place. I pray for them to go into realms they have never been in before. Lord, let the Bible become their delight. I pray that there would not be a formula but a desire, a passion of fire that burns on the inside of them. Lord, let this be such a fiery passion that no foe would be able to withstand it. Let supernatural strength come upon them.

Lord, bless every winner who is reading this. Speak to them. Direct them as they seek Your face, in Jesus' name.

Amen.

Made in the USA
Middletown, DE
27 September 2023

39343409R00056